Downfall
of the
Straight Line

ARROWSMITH⟫⫡
PRESS

Downfall
of the
Straight Line

Charles O. Hartman

Downfall of the Straight Line
Charles O. Hartman

ISBN: 979-8-9879241-9-8

Boston — New York — San Francisco — Baghdad
San Juan — Kyiv — Istanbul — Santiago, Chile
Beijing — Paris — London — Cairo — Madrid
Milan — Melbourne — Jerusalem — Darfur

11 Chestnut St.
Medford, MA 02155

arrowsmithpress@gmail.com
www.arrowsmithpress.com

The fifty-eighth Arrowsmith book was typeset & designed by Ezra Fox
for Askold Melnyczuk & Alex Johnson in Baskerville font

for Martha Collins

CONTENTS

I

II

III

I

A Glorious Sky

The clouds look proud
because we have to gape so far up.

Really they're confused and disconcerted:
herded, riven, with not much time

as clouds. How fine
that they up there

take after us: waiting, demented by brevity,
driven askew, evaporating.

(But what levity! What a view!)

Sweet Almond

Lest the great shout that is spring
happen wholly without us
this unhappy year, we walk

out under buds and birdsongs,
sometimes in the same high tree,
and we look up earnestly

the names of both, to name them
to each other, if only
over the phone, or leave them

at each other's distant door:
a vase of names, a quiet
bouquet of would-be touches.

It troubles, some, to fathom how
lucky we are that words come
(maybe with a thumb-sized glimpse

on a thumb-smudged screen)
so close to satisfying
the needs that make us creatures.

Enough of this human stuff—
this closet, window chatter.
The tree that accosted me

today, with its five-fold pale
petals in tens of thousands
and serrated leaves, gave me

a message to pass along.
As near as I can recall,
this was it. Oh, and this too:

come out, all the way out,
not out of words—bring the words—
but into the shouts of birds.

Dead Tree in the Back Yard

You aren't mine. A lot line
jinks across the mind's map
between us. When you fall
you won't befall my roof.

Scrupulous woodpeckers
sculpt you: they have the time,
you've got the goods. Summer
cardinals your bare bones.

As turkey roost, you're swayed.
Coyote trots below.
Those who farmed here, clearing
all else, made you wolf tree.

Across upright years, your
attitude has prospered
like a reputation
to make me admire death.

I found tapes: my father
teaching, not quite in my
voice, not not, saying things
I'd say now. I come to

my own attention, like
the osprey—sudden, pale,

erect and feat-feathered,
head turned earthward in high

study—who selected
this minute in autumn
to settle a moment,
lean, spread, and sail away.

Remembered Scars

On one thigh the white arc—
where a wire fence,
climbed in eighth grade

to retrieve a soccer ball, exacted
penalty not deep but visibly
stubborn—stood out

against the pallor
for two decades
or three: when did I last

see it and apologize
to the leg or for the leg
as its custodian?

And then where my knife
whittling the image
of a boat slipped

and turned up a flap of flesh
just above the other knee,
the knee declared

in sun and pool and bed
for more years than I can recall
the knife, the slip.

How many years
can be recalled, scored
as they are? In skin,

collagen fibers
strew. A scar is where,
repairing, they align. A time ago

I saw the marks. Behold
me, immaculate, bereft,
outliving them.

Same

Drying your back with a towel
for example: to do it while
remembering doing it
a thousand times in the past
three years, tens over decades,
holding the two in the one
thought, if thought is the word for what

being is like: this is not useful,
if use is what you want, but the feel
of terrycloth's rougher side
against skin you know
is naked, though you can't see it,
has the advantage of being

now. It's like practicing your daily
daily scales, and halfway down
letting one note sing
while you ask all the other fingers
what they think.

The Pianos

All graceful instruments are known.
—The Grateful Dead

Amid so much sleep,
we remember the waking phrases:
iterations bored or rapturous,
resounding hours, rehearsals
of the opulent impromptu, the melody
sketched by a right hand
once and let drop.

We almost remember the hundred hands'
thousands of operations
fashioning us for the sleek
showroom, the dim loft,
the highly favored dorm,
the not-quite-defunct
club: solarium, atrium.

Among us we have taught
some children what they are.

Whether we're Grand (the satin
titan with mammoth underbite)
or Upright (but *spinet* is an ugly name),
everyone has a fallboard eyelid.

We all need work. My felts
haven't been pricked for years.
The sostenuto's flabby.
A long life can be ghastly, last
decades in an untunable basement:
peeling, untouched
even into noise.

Once on a loading dock
Steinway CD 318 and I
passed back to back:
Gould's own, on loan to Evans.
This was before the fall.
Another I knew stroked Tatum's fingers,
then Peterson's—a junker by then,
with a fresh coat of paint.

When Monk's burned, everyone
went dumb for a day.

When I first came home
under the round window—
even as I heard the truck's
pads and dollies tucked back in
while guys flexed shoulders for the next—
on that still first morning
I answered Bach with Bach, and when at last
she stood and away from me
to speak to some others,
I knew her heart was mine.

A Moment as Home

Before we knew we know how the tune goes,
we heard the bare ways *up-and-down*,
fast-and-slow, as if it were Greek
in a Roman ear, or we were fry
trying to do as fish, or dance
were meant for four deaf feet apiece. By now

it's a steady shower on our shoulders,
warm rain we won't shelter from,
like the astonishment of sex, or time
read for a moment as home,
or a thought that halts thought. Time to say
we knew it all along? Meantime

it was a song of sorts, a currency: words we knew.
You sang it, everyone sang it. We gave it our days.
Our children had already heard
everything we heard. We tried not to gape,
catching a lilt that meant us so much good
we could taste it, red beans & rice.

It turned to something we see through
the way the air clears to a field of stars
or a face suddenly gleams free
of the cloud of habit,
something we hear through
like the story

I thought to tell you the other day, the day
the heavens strutted up and made
a charade we barely saw among chores and budgets,
dust and the broken sash. The sky—our sky!—
was ear-splitting cross-purpose, worse & worse.
Remember the *sturm* & all that *drang*. Why should it take

so long to say this? When we were young—
when even the sixties were young—
they tried to kill us to save us
from wickedness or out of mutual
fear or sheer pushbutton fuckup. Then
we learned the story

is not a song: so not the song. So here
we lie in a light the moon cannot account for,
in a wealth of silence, in truth as in this thick
dark blanket with the embroidered stars,
up to our necks in mercy,
without a tale.

Choosing Sides

Not to go to bed
but to stay the night there,
we have to work out
who gets which.

Whose habit's stronger
decides, except
in the happy case
where bents agree.

This is universal—yet we have
no common language
for which is which.
North or East won't do,

nearer the bathroom and
beside the lamp fall
short of the particular
variety among beds.

We'd like to say just *right* or *left*,
but whose, and lying
face up or down? We figure
all this geography

out, as we must.
It may take talk—
all to the good,
being what we do best.

Moon Light

Bless her who blessed us with
this gift, this bauble, pharos-

paraphrase of Earth's,
our satellight, a bubble

to make your room a fable
of seeing through the night.

This 3D-printed globe,
crater by crater true,

minutely rough—as is,
no doubt, the original

to the soft hand of God—
hankers to show us us.

Who knew it was so light?
—that clinker in the sky,

to rest its ounces on
a wireframe cube of basswood.

Who knew it had a button
to switch from gold to rare

blue, and dim it too?
We said this afternoon,

looking ahead to night,
Last up turns out the moon!

We Know

The time will come, we know, when one of us,
catching a summer chill,
takes on the fulltime, lifelong chore of being ill;
or something sidesteps all that fuss,
some blow we won't have leisure to discuss—
one absent-minded footfall on a hill,
or too close to a cougar's kill.
Soon or late, one will prove the obvious.

The other, paperwork and speeches done, will come
home to the thought of home, wanting a drink,
a kiss, not to be there another year or twenty.
In that too spacious minimum,
at least for a time there will be time to think
back over plenty.

Constellations

On my back at the physical
therapist's office I consider
why in the tiles overhead

the spray of holes
echoes a starfield photograph:
the scatter of them,

their mix of sizes—not
the geometric drill of old
lunchrooms, but designed

to absorb the manifold
frequencies that make noise
noise. She coaxes

my body to relax
against the brouhaha
of nerves dictating strict

configurations which the skeleton
accepts by deforming. We taxed ourselves
to give ourselves

a better Hubble:
Webb: the bureaucrat
who took to the moon

four guys, none of them me
for reasons not restricted
to my back. It's less about

taxes than about being
absorbed. Her next-to-silent
Classical murmurs on. To find a star

that moves (*planetum*, comet, death
-dealing asteroid) we use a blink
comparator: two plates of the same

sky, a stereoscope, a button
for back and forth. The speck that jumps
is not of the Fixed Stars. The sky

maps well-studied stresses, and we
pick out the squeaky wheel. Did the moon
squeak? We who wished upon

going did—and in those same years marched
for budgets for the underclass.
Our motto: never

zero-sum! Among muscles,
when one wins
and another loses,

so do all. All noise
canceled, we can't tell
that we're not deaf.

Crab Nebula

A.D. 1054

When I upon the rise of gravity
threw violently around me the gaudiest shawl
the universe has room for; when I turned

so hard on myself and fast that only flesh
substantial as mine could cohere, a self so
concentrated that whatever crossed me

I menaced with devouring; when I tortured
the very place I turned in, scene of my
so recent, long-assembled, glorious

undoing, and for an hour hesitated
on the brink of taking all my brilliance
in out of this time entirely—

then I glanced
once more at what I'd thrown aside and saw
devised in that stuff of my disaster

tissue of worlds, blood of minute beasts,
endlessly raveling strew of circumstance,
histories strange to mine in everything

but plot: all of it certain, all for now still
blazing away in such incipience
that those far off would strain and say, *a cloud.*

From Where You Are

1. Moon

From the north end of Earth,
to see what the moon's becoming,
look at its right side:
bright there and it brightens,

dark and it wanes. At last, it is
new, and nothing to us—
though nervous with ingratitude
we mutter like huddled turkeys

spells and tales to say
it's *always* wandered off like this;
really we and our little doggie
are on a roll. Yet every year

we push another inch or two apart.
Once she is wholly gone,
no tides to rinse our sore shores,
we'll give our kids nostalgic names

like *Crescent*, little
Gibbous the hunchback, teenage
Waxing, dreamy *Tranquility*.
Eons farther on, our Dad the Sun

swells red and swallows us
stones and nematodes and all.
No Zeus to make him
vomit us back.

For now,
we sing together
them dirty blues—
Oh didn't we ramble!

2. Compass

Hold your watch
horizontal. Point the hour hand
at the sun. Halfway between
there and twelve

is south. If your watch
has no hands, draw a face
on paper, mark the hour,
and divide. Half

because your hour hand,
if you have one, runs
twice as fast as the sun.
If however you are in

the southern parts of Earth,
point twelve at the sun, and south's
halfway to the hour.
Most of us are in the north,

though more will be in the Global South—
the money line
running way above the equator.
I should have said this

also about the moon:
if you are south,
read *left* for *right*.
If you're between

tropics, to work
the trick with the watch you need to know
which half of the year
you're in. Noon ranges.

3. Rainbow

To see one, on a world
that is, as I have mentioned
elsewhere, near
the triple point of water,

look away from the sun:
west in the morning,
east in the evening,
particularly after a storm,

when the day behind you is clear sky
and you look onto dark clouds
whose rain has left your air
full of invisibly small

prisms, packets
of facets for light
to play among and flee and so
display. The bigger,

the more red. It will be
forty-two degrees
across, call it
half of half

of half the earth's edge—
unless you fly
high enough to see
the circle whole:

every rainbow
being a ring whose lower part's
hidden below the horizon
you make by being there.

Grove

Your tarred lot has lapped
nearly to where our knuckles clutch loam.
We stand in tall thought, never lost,
remembering the rubbish of underbrush
and the decent pond before you.

Here before you,
we to whom is not assigned
the task of shivering ourselves warm
shiver without the disease of reasons
more or less in any wind.

Who knows the will of water?
whether in cut glass scabbards on the twigs
that make our early birds' feet skid
or withheld for weeks in high cloud—
once locked rushing in the phloem

it bears us up to bearing.
We are its children.
Where a thicket was,
you thinned
to us, who stood just where you wanted

trees. In puddles
where your clomping galoshes
trouble the sky,

our gaunt
reflections ramify.

We bow above. Come in among us:
we'll drip down your napes.
Not part of the old world now
we are the old world.
We still breathe for you.

II

Jet Lag

Cowslips in a shotglass. An awkward gift
is landscape grander than the grasping eye.
The wholly whelming sea. A butterfly-
bright sun, Greek clouds like summer yachts adrift
above. Below, the race *is* to the swift.
Bad dream: to end with just an alibi,
with instruments as blunt as honesty
and virtues as peripheral as thrift.

Deep night. I'm up to check the balcony.
Orion's staring in, the Pleiades
glimmer not looked at straight. I look straight on
the big dark, balancing fear, ecstasy,
and breeze-blown robe-silk tickling at my knees.
A new world! and just when the old one's gone.

Waking Nowhere

When I wake I wonderfully
can't tell where I am.
Do I have a neighbor

who keeps chickens?
That scrape's a rake
or a whetstone wielded slowly.

The hiss is tires
not on dirt—but pavement
wet or dry? The universals

are particular: if the road's dry
the tires are a little flat.
A yowl's a baby's or a cat's,

but two is cats. Two birds
debate sunshine. No drone
of small planes. The notes

sinter into a chord.
I rise and go robed to the balcony
and find the stained cement

of the opposite roof
familiar as an old drunk
after the bar chucks everybody out;

same pickup down in the square,
dead transmission in its ribbed bed.
The blue house remains blue.

Sound can't hold still.
Sound is now, here. It speaks beat,
the mother heart. Oh, sight

just *is* that way—near, far.
Mountains on the one hand,
sea on the other.

Donkey in the Air

While I stood as usual,
as usual they added stones
to the back of the cart
presumably, presumably

behind the axle, so,
not suddenly but at some tipping point,
the market square began to fall away.
Look at that bell tower.

Who would have guessed.
Meanwhile the chest, supposed to hang
from the firm arch of the spine,
ached in harness. The clapper lolled.

If I've been sure of anything
it's footing. Now I find
less traction than a swimming dog.
Could try what the birds do. No.

You're gaping. I would too.
I have a couple of ideas
which unfortunately involve hands.
You capped fool with the camera:

why not scurry to unload stones,
return me to the useful earth?

No, this is too much fun. Snap on,
develop, print, make a postcard

to amuse your tourists
from Pakistan to Naples,
till it slips into the fist
of a Greek who will do a trick

to transpose my hung,
ridiculously elevated body
into a picture of his own
village to shame the locals.

Then one of you can turn it into words,
also good for bandying about—
always glad to be of whatever service,
in the quarry of your decades.

At last, since nobody wants
to deal with me dead, somebody starts
lifting off counterweights.
No plummet,

just hind legs, a little kicking,
watch the tail, then fore,
back in the belonging dust.
That's settled.

In Front of a Shop

Her dress swells in the wind
and her hair waving in it
resembles the tendrils of bougainvillea,
which in Greek is *bougainvillea*.
She stares, or is meant
to stare, at nothing,
which signifies something interior.

She stands as if astonished.
Sometimes her whole body
shivers stiffly in the designer breeze.
The swivel of her right wrist,
a line like a bracelet of black thread,
is turned in the downward orientation
that says: I am imagining

something bulbous I might seize for pleasure
or power, such as a gearshift.
Her left hand is hidden
behind the scarf thrown over her shoulder,
a shade to compliment her dress and looking
as if it ought to tickle.
She can shrug it off

no better than she can shy away
from the shop front and her sister
across the doorway, lolling in a more

deeply pensive, downcast attitude.
For a while the owner
stood by them, still (except for her cigarette)
as the girls on the Acropolis.

Skate

Their foot shall slide in due time.

—Deuteronomy 32:35

You make your friends call you Magic Mike
but your nollie & kickflip needed work,
your mongo-foot & shove-it. Now, downhill,
since helmets deafen and throw you off, you're busted:

prone and blank.
Around the fair turn glides the cyclist,
not fast, but dazzled glad with the blooming day,
her lover's train due soon—and at the spectacle

of your sorry carcass brakes
herself over the bars.
The smeared knee will swell to immobility for days.
You startled her into hurt. I could kill you

off here—your bad dream
fresh off the train from Dodge—
yet not run the clock back, brace
your fidgety foot, or stand in her path

half-seen, ghostly-semaphoric,
nor check the cherry flower boughs set out
to charm her interim. For this day this
god quits. Just watch yourself.

Peninsular

The fishing boat motors in & draws water after,
the water spreads & loses memory of the boat
& returns to gazing at the sky

though it can be distracted by wind.
So the soul, etc. On the third morning
after a day of dividing water from water

before any sun could render limpid the niceties of geometry
there seemed to be a need for land, & if so why not plants
& so the sorry invention of reproductive strategies.

Even with a day aside for astronomy
the world grew dense with things.
As for swallows' tails, wakes set in obsidian,

who could compare them, so swift to veer,
to the eldest curse, which comes causeless.
Over this promontory with its regrettable neck of land

soar the blue-gray jets trailing cones of thunder,
hard in the high deep to tell from gulls,
except that they never correct for updrafts with a shrug

but plunge straight past bluffs & waters toward a nest
no more useful to the future than mine—
stone wedged on stone at the cave's maw.

The path down to the washing-place
chitters with cries in aid of fornication,
such as make the whole body itch, the pleasure to assuage it

rich though a little wretched. Honey comes
to those who shelter bees. Thank then the astringent sea,
even the sky & all who sail in her, the wretched, rich

land, too, of perplexing thorn. If all this is to end
timely, a tent rolled into a traveling bag,
if the curse's calculation be exacted out to zero,

then the void unfolds again as at first, & this time
with the one scribed track of a swallow forever
forgotten behind it.

Peripheral Vision

An optometrist told my father
his could have made him a great
truck driver: "They test for that."

Around the curve of the century
I see him at it: a *Violent Road*
volunteer, long-haul and lonely.

I see him as peripterist,
owner of an Athens corner
news-and-sundries hut

vital to daily life,
the neighborhood's central intelligence,
a veteran among veterans,

the wounded and the war widows;
ensconced like a fighter pilot
behind ranks of magazines and chips,

bus tickets and sunglasses,
books with the spines outward,
goods on the outer slopes

heaped at the angle of repose,
the least expensive the most visible;
hunched on the stool in his two-meter cave,

room for one,
eyes on everything,
manning the panopticon,

watchful of wares,
purchase-port on the swarming street
with side-slats to guard

first and third base;
shelves inside piled to the apex
with condoms and cigarettes,

guide books in the less demanded languages:
everything in reach.
At the back, the hatch.

It must have been my father
who took me to see *Violent Road* —
my mother wouldn't've. Or was it

The Wages of Fear, French with subtitles,
which *Violent Road* remade?
In the age of knowledge,

no way to know;
no one to tell me.
I see myself, son and heir

and near double in spirit, as in want
of those leather blinders
for a horse between shafts

to keep it focused,
keep it from being spooked;
if only not to remember only I

wander out here, street-legal,
with no commodities, footloose
or as they call it free.

Assembly Square

Nafplio

Not peace, but a picture of peace,
or of where peace might touch down
or spring forth, whatever peace does
to arrive: pines and palms,
neat public polygons of local stone,
benches, pavers grooved
for a season when wet stone
breaks ankles,
all below the long ridge
fortified so grandly the second time

Venetians tried to hold the town
and heroes had names like Turk-Eater.
Any Turks now, migrants and refugees,
stay low to avoid being eaten
by anything quicker than economics.
Tourism can't fix everything,
as Satan, once Lucifer (*Myself*
am hell) was first to recognize
(*nor am I out of it*). The Square's
citizens come and go: the mother

pedaling steadily uphill
as the child in back gazes everywhere,
the six old men sagging

in chairs in the café in the sun,
the mothers and daughters lumbering
bag-laden from the week's market.
Doves hoot in 5/4, smaller
self-important birds chatter together,
shreds of talk drift like smoke from the café,
the chuckle of a starting car

parries the slow surf of a passing one.
Here I can sit idle, crossing my legs
which men don't much do in Greece
because it might suggest
balls smaller than cantaloupes.
The biggest building across the green
—headquarters of the neo-
Nazi Golden Dawn—is not very big.
Everything to scale, everything
true to Euclid. I am not sure

what constitutes peace,
but a mind either freed of darkness
or filled with light, a light
not very much different from what floods
this square according to its own laws,
the straight lines among all surfaces
and the tinier adjustments that are color,
would seem like a good beginning:
an orange in the grass
in the shadow of a palm.

Economies

1: Rates of Exchange

At the end of your stay,
when the entropy of change—
you amass it by the scrupulous pound

but won't fuss in spending—has rendered
metal a weight against your thigh,
cargo that crowds your passport,

so that you wrap the lot in a sheet
of substantial hotel paper, a second
crosswise for surety, for the man who has

asked for it daily, need crazy with hope,
whom you will find by your café
snug among cypresses,

add, among the rubble,
a guinea or golden
ducat or whatever's

current. Would you confer
your load of trouble
and none of what breeds it?

2: Clock Work

A few coins a day
replenishes the jar
to a pound, to half a stone,

till need or the mere weight of it
goads, and you trade
the lot for paper:

one of the year's escapements:
—that big pivot up near the moon—
millennium pendulum

disturbed—magnet in the cabinet—
vicious whims in the jet stream—
beta decays partitioning worlds:

something lets go
and one of the globe's bins
tilts and troops spill down the continent

to choke the other end
leaving a trail of bone and burned hair:
history's broad smear

gummed up again.
That penny saved. That dollar
so easy in its billfold.

This Distance

Aegina

If you think you could hear the heat,
it's probably cicadas you're remembering.
At this distance you don't feel it,
don't be ridiculous, but you put together
an angle of vision—steeply uphill—
and the raw rub of a backpack
you gave up years ago, and crushed sage
and thyme, and you are as there
as you habitually are where you are.

Down below, the sea must be a bathtub,
so small are the boats, the smacks and ketches,
the ferry leaving along its long curve.
The notion that you could be there and here
is a difficult and necessary dilemma:
as soon as you try to assemble words for it
and realize you've taken them from two languages,
you've lost it again and hold it as fast
as anything, any moment, you can grasp.

Flag

You have to mine and refine,
smelt, roll and extrude,
before you can forge a pole
to erect in the cold
to stick your tongue to.

You could imagine
from first principles
a beehive-furnace and by trial
fix the temperature for the work:
no calculating till you've done it
twice. Each try takes a tree
you fell and dismantle,
haul and split
and stack in there and light.
Wait it out.
Too cold and the ore stays
stingy clots. Too hot
and the metal dribbles away—
unless the heat's so high
it evaporates, but this requires
a nuclear blast or getting too near
a sun, and these entail
skills and equipment you won't
work out for a while.

In between you learn
to pick the right rocks
—lots of the greeny ones
and a handful of these black crystals
from islands so far and frigid
you may as well invent trade,
which will take sails and keels
and the twining of miles of rope.

In the end you'll have a thing
you can hang something from
to salute, to plant
on another planet,
forget in the rain or bring down
to drape a casket.
The lanyard will have its tantrum in the wind.
So forge ahead, best foot.
The stars have held their breath
long enough.

The Minefield

I

In the hospital after so strangely
and to his chagrin not dying,
my father scrawled me a note.
In the night, his feet
being cold, he had written
(presumably on that same pad)
to ask the nurse for sox,
and she had patiently explained
that sex was not among her duties.
Puzzling out his writing, I could tell
he thought this a very funny joke on himself.
Not up to sharing it
like a buddy at the end of the War
in Germany not far
from his ancestors' village
where the two of them, lost,
slept exhausted on a hillside
which morning revealed
as a minefield, I could only ask,
Who but a ball team
spells it with an x?

II

That night
I turn on the television
and see him on a panel
to discuss trigger-squeeze.
He can't talk,

and the moderator
fidgets and glances at the camera.
A commercial extols
the taste of whale steak:
like butter. When we come back

the lights gleam from the wheels and rails
of his mobile office.
On my own ill-engineered stool
I straighten a paperclip
more and more precisely.

III

My father's stroke—which left his mind
alone, froze half his body, took
his walk—stole him and left behind
a statue to my father's look,

husk of his voice. In school I learned
to call this irony. The grim
vision that calls it just, well-earned,
inevitable, I learned from him.

He'd say to say God struck him dumb—
not countless cigarettes and seas
of coffee—would be to succumb
to comforting hypotheses.

In another dream sonhood invokes
I burst in out of anywhere
to rattle off a chain of jokes
and dance around his silver chair.

Uncanny Daddy

When you were three
kiddo
for reasons lost to time
I shaved off beard and mustache,

and when I came downstairs
you smiled
the way you still do
at strangers, till I said

something and you knew my voice
and burst into tears.
Alien is OK
until it springs

from behind someone you know.
It was almost another
year before I left. Kiddo,
it was never you.

Lies

The first time I was on television,
and about the last,
I sat in a row of kids
from my school I guess,
each aimed at in turn
to say Hi Mom Hi

Dad Hi Everybody.
The host was Buffalo
Biff or Bart, or some
such ersatz grownup.
This was St. Louis, but the sponsor
was Washington State

apples—and there they were,
the more-than-Midwestern, ruby pyramid
of slim-pointed bases
hand-fitted to mountain-pass crests,
between us and the camera.
At home, I divulged

how the backs of the apples
versus the gleaming front of the pile
were bruised and
maybe I said wormy. The story
was appreciated, the moral
clear to us all.

Gait

1.

We get over ground
by going over
the ground. Wait,
what? Or staying
over it—simple as that. Upright
as that, as
long as we can.
Or so.

2.

The classification of gaits
begins from the left hindlimb.
Beyond the sequence
are symmetries
and beats.

3.

The earth
waits for us: we wait
to welcome it. We trust
it will as well.

4.

Petty pace. Through
our paces. It is the pace
that kills. *To be buried*

in the myddell pace
before the high crosse.

5.
A lizard or turtle
which has no diaphragm
and breathes by expanding its whole body
with the very muscles
used for the undulation of walking
cannot at the same time
breathe and move.

6.
The amble—between
walk and gallop, if the horse
is of that parentage (gene
DMRT3)—has gratified many
in the saddle, whatever their mounts
might think. From Hittites
through our Middle Ages, amblers were
prized for smoothness on long rides, and are.
Two beasts
at once, like us:
the front feet trot
while the rear walk.

7.
Bipeds walk or run—
second by second the ground
keeps track of us, or we fly
minutely—

8.
or hop, like kangaroos.
From there to flight is far,
far, but we have
time, because we make time
who can mark time,
pacing.

9.
Before chronometers, Galileo
clocked his inclined planes'
evidence on gravity
by singing madrigals. We know
how the tune is meant
to go.

10.
The sole presses earth
so briefly—most of the step
taken up with putting down
and levering there to lift again—
we can hardly say
we set foot anywhere.

11.
Since it requires
meaning to, only
humans
skip.

You Too, Bro?

Whatever the crow
recovers, it isn't
dignity. Mobbed, jayed,

she flaps to a backup branch
& resettles feathers.
If she's still there,

pal, it's not to brood
—nowhere in view, really,
to move to, wide as her prospect

is. No point
regurgitating old quarrels
in a world picked clean.

Who killed whom
i' th' Capitol? Does it matter
at this remove?

The sun is fire
& gives fire
everything. This glittering world

will kill us all.
If I'm still here
I'm gathering

what light I can. If not,
I did. (& what jays,
mate, drive you?)

III

Autumn Ordinance

Just as, when you keep watch
on the ground ahead of where your boots
kick up the leaves, the path
goes vague and blurred, while

if you lift your eyes the far
reach of the trail comes lucid
as map; so when you look
at tomorrow through next year,

the way, otherwise
so tangled and burdensome,
clears. And if the leaves
are, as they likely are,

fallen from the trees around you,
then you get to look
deeper into things
than spring allowed.

The Eye Gone Still

As when you stall, absent,
before a pond, gray water
among gray trees, beige pond-stones,
nothing—until by doing nothing
you startle into visibility
the heron now bending down and up-
turning a wealth of wing
to rise out of it and away;

or when that trick of light
gleams into question a lover's eye
where nothing shone but certainty,
and suddenly you're bound to be
bedded for hours in talk,
preposterous hypotheses
like vying fireworks, meaning
splashing like paint around an upended studio:

that's what they must look like,
our deaths, when they come upon us,
or we on them as it seems we must:
a sudden change in plans for the afternoon.
How do you take surprise parties? Delight?
Outrage? Despondency? These streams
pool for the eye to linger on
when you have a moment.

Pas de Deux

This flower depends
on a fly that eats the guts

of dying bees, so it emits
a scent assiduously near

to bees' fear pheromone.
The fly dithers—no bee!—

but then descends
and is penned

for days inside the cone
knee-deep in pollen

until the flower withers,
then gropes away to find—

the flower hopes—
another of its kind.

As Some Thresholds Can Be Crossed Only by Dancing

what's weightless
what most
aptly becomes smoke
what anyone forgets at first sight
daylight's dark matter

that corner of the pond
anyone looks away from
eye's corner
the one way to see it

sleep's eye's all corner

shoreline
copper shoots
crowding out old green
a flurry of insects
unable to tell
themselves from motes
plot light against gravity
for inquisition
of water grasses

all unsayables
hover equally

anyone awake
watches the compression
of afternoon to fire

here are keys but to what kingdom

Briefcase

When she set in to die
she took nothing.
Which is how to do it.
It took a year.

A policeman called me.
He let me choose.
I climbed the stairs to see
her open eyes.

Then went another year.
While she was dead
I dragged her life around
in a water-

proof blue nylon briefcase
to attorneys
and administrators
and accountants.

Then a dozen of us
bore her body,
compact as live but no
longer limber,

clear-bagged in a black box,
down to the sea.
In a line, in silence,
in turn we took

handfuls, and let them go.
And that was that.

Reckoning

The poor   the rich   the living
the fleet of foot   the well-loved
the unguarded   the alert
the soon to be elect
the insomniac   the deaf

the hugely endowed
the violent   the never
satisfied   the young   the not
broken   the swift to judge   the
easy or eager to please

the mad   the not bad   the un-
bearably beautiful   the
unironically faithful
the born   the suddenly lone
the finished by divine fire

the unfired   the still   the still
ready   the undone   the mere
dead   the inaudible dead
the nearly   the unaccountable
the dead beyond reckoning

The Birthdays of the Dead

It is an affront in their land
to remind someone of that first
exile because they recollect

the sojourn with terror still and
regret the loss of it. All those
dawns, roads, splinters, whiskies and hard
chairs, all that fucking and eating

and talk, talk, talk. They never talk
since it takes tongue and breath. All that
breathing! they say inside themselves
when the memorial comes round.
Well out of that cadence! they say

all day. No more of those little
amnesias, the sleeps! Now they have
more than all the time in the world.
Someone just across the border

has tied two fingers together
with black thread, not to forget, till
nightfall and the time to cut it.

Rescue

If I dream a bird on the floor
sick or injured, maybe able
to be gathered in a towel
and taken somewhere to somebody—

once day comes and I go
off into it, it makes no sense
to wonder about the bird.
So responsibility

ends in dreams. Or does the bird,
whether or not I wonder?
If I don't dream

myself, who does? Home again,
confronting the mirror,
I press the towel into my face.

Lost on a Road I Know

Heavens, I recognize the place, I know it!
—Bishop

Dreadful as getting here can be,
lost I mean, the deepening

perplexity, the should-I-turn
that way, or back, the did-I-miss,

this is a sweet
shock, this

waking to amazement:
that 76 in brass

on the cedarwood mailbox,
that short steep with a turn up top,

the holly bush
too dark to bespeak summer.

First I am nowhere, then
somewhere, then between points

on a mind's winding line, a path
all turns and dips

and rises, a road
with an end, where I was

going. Elsewhere
on the level

the car set in motion
idle & automatic

advances without will.
But being here, accumulating

surprise, requires
countless accelerations:

gathering, gathering
a particular angle of steering wheel,

this oak with two left branches,
that stone wall's Morse of mosses,

lichen calligraphy—
until the name of the road

throws itself in the way,
and our little life

rounds on its own sleep.
To have come this way, come

all this way, to be
lost! redeems the way.

Never Mind

I open my old copy
of *Names of the Lost.*

A card falls out.
The return address

is clear, and the name—
a firm hand. And the face,

enough for me to see the chin, the cloud
of red hair, the almost invisible

auburn fur over her body.
The card says "back in town"

and lists plans for the next year.
Postscript: "Never mind."

Now I remember months before,
she phoned

to ask to meet—to call
it off, I could see

when she walked in.
I assented. I took her hand

and led her outside to see the summer
willow shimmering in monarchs.

Later this card.
Later still,

in a new age, it becomes
easy to learn

she died a dozen years back.
Between, she taught, edited

a book on women miners,
married, divorced. This

is me recalling
our never-quite-a-story.

How she saw it I will
not be able

to ask. I want to believe
I would have.

The Close

After those years of worship at her skin
and swearing to and by and at her sway,
turning at last Actaeon, wolfed, at bay,
I came out through the thick into the thin.

What passed for me passed on. Surviving twin,
I learned another, single strain to play:
to howl at stone and hear delay decay
and drown the name of damage in mere din.

Say that I slept and woke another man.
Or say the cleft where the pooled time escapes
began to open when the close began.
Or just that love, which falls like desert rain,
tears its arroyos' ragged walls and shapes
the land, and blooms it, and is gone again.

A Threshold

When the last of these words fades
where will you go? You'll step
outside into the fog
that buried the road years ago,
where sound dies after a few yards
and everything smells mulched.
Not that nobody's there—
people stumble around selling certificates,
grooming their lizards. Only they don't speak
or make anything or remember.
They breathe fog.
                              Or is the fog
inside? Maybe the fields run,
miles of loam, all the way to a city
that gleams like a bubble
and hums like choirs. Maybe
people live out there forever.

Penny Bright

I

Some yellow flowers
you walk past with a woman
who knows names of flowers.
Don't want to get it wrong.
A head

you cradle in unaccountably
weak arms.
Ideas about hair, blown
carelessly by a breeze that can
afford to be careless. Hair

bunched in your hands
over your sleeping face. A voice,
Fuck it, you don't know
what *it* it means. Your voice.
Some pieces of money

from your clogged pocket
called *change*. Unaccountable. Faces
foreign as yours, the strange
denominations.
Dime.

II

The pool ball rolls
on a tune of three sounds
ending in the familiar
kiss with another—*chick*—
anyone would recognize,
after the cushion spoke
of something hard
bumped against something padded.
Before, the struck
ball rolling away on felt
over slate, the thunder
coming before
and under things.

III

Call it the moon. O moon—
If the moon were no farther away
than death you would hold it
in your hand that shakes in such

dis-ease, as if holding
a yellow flower still stiff with stemmed water, as if
all were not well.
Call it well. Call death

a melodrama posed beside some crag,
wanting to play Go.

Flowers, or another hand with flowers.
You've forgotten the rules,

ideas about territory and violation. Stones,
some like the full moon, some the new.
You believe in endings and want to know
where it will end.

IV

Name *daffodil* from name
asphodel, flower of the dead begun with *de*
from French: dead who need
flowers more than you do, with more
time to account for. Sound
of a train that trundles
past the back window,

a purpose that ignores you.
An arm thrust blindly through silence
around a shoulder: there you are.
Jonquil that is *junco* near enough.
You mine your pocket, bring up
a nickel, which if it were made of nickel.
Someone is watching

by the flowers, death
taking a shape in air,
mouthing names. A mouth
shaping your name.

In sleep her leg,
bent then extended into space sliced free of time,
your time, jerked like a dreaming dog's.

Something stirs. Time enough to ask what
tomorrow: from a root, to flicker,
referring to "dim
states of illumination"
as in the Latin for "unmixed wine"
that yields
mere.

V

Never mind death: consider his rich
great-niece humiliation. Consider
Vespasian ("I will not kill
a dog that barks at me"), conqueror
of Judea. To test tales of his new
Dead Sea he chose
soldiers who couldn't swim
and bound their hands.

VI

Outside the window you face at dinner
the light

through most of spring

shows the pristine tree:

a round fact of cogent green, growing
older. As it grows

older it presents a less clear, less
spherical image. You can't want

to cut it down.
How many years to watch?

VII

The dead are farther away. Less, more.

That little hitch in the voice.

Dream is a makeshift.

VIII

There's a name for this and if I knew it
it could stand, bright penny, clear
as *juniper*

beside the hemlock, dark
masses both, otherwise.
Obsession won't do, obsession

won't do. Abroad, once, at dawn
when I stepped outside the *dacha*
in that settlement of ex-generals

sleeping off the vodka
that kept me up, I heard
from the front lines of endless evergreen

the cuckoo
for the first time, and knew her
because she spoke her name.

I Made a City

I made a city walled in wood
And set it in the sea.
I named the flood our gravest good
And surety.

We watched the clouds that are and are
And read the wind for way,
Living the near to learn the far
Of the last day.

Storm-rain's cuneiform on wave
Recorded our long lore
So all we gave we might yet have,
If we reached shore.

I settled us on the tall hill
Where wisdom rests her sole,
And the owl lit on the old sill
And made us whole.

ACKNOWLEDGMENTS

My thanks to the following publications, in which some of these poems appeared:

Copper Nickel: "Donkey in the Air" (as "The Donkey in the Air")

Louisville Review: "Remembered Scars," "Sweet Almond," "You Too, Bro?"

On the Seawall: "Constellations"

A Poetry Pedagogy for Teachers: Reorienting Classroom Literacy Practices (ed. Maya Pindyck and Ruth Vinz), Bloomsbury, 2022: "Same," "The Pianos"

Plume: "The Birthdays of the Dead," "Dead Tree in the Back Yard," "Gait," "In Front of a Shop" (as "Enthralled"), "The Minefield," "Uncanny Daddy"

The Red Letters: "A Glorious Sky," "Moon Light," "We Know"

Salamander: "Rescue"

Seneca Review: "Assembly Square," "Autumn Ordinance," "Briefcase," "A Moment as Home," "Peninsular" (as "Peninsula"), "Penny Bright," "This Distance," "Waking Nowhere"

spoKe7: "Crab Nebula," "The Eye Gone Still," "Lost on a Road I Know"

Charles O. Hartman has published seven previous collections, including *New & Selected Poems* (Ahsahta); a textbook (*Verse: An Introduction to Prosody*, Wiley-Blackwell); and three books of critical prose (*Free Verse*, *Jazz Text*, and *Virtual Muse*). He co-edited  the volume on Wendy Battin for the Unsung Masters series. He is Professor and Poet in Residence Emeritus at Connecticut College. He plays jazz guitar.

Books by

ARROWSMITH
PRESS

Girls by Oksana Zabuzhko

Bula Matari/Smasher of Rocks by Tom Sleigh

This Carrying Life by Maureen McLane

Cries of Animals Dying by Lawrence Ferlinghetti

Animals in Wartime by Matiop Wal

Divided Mind by George Scialabba

The Jinn by Amira El-Zein

Bergstein
edited by Askold Melnyczuk

Arrow Breaking Apart by Jason Shinder

Beyond Alchemy by Daniel Berrigan

Conscience, Consequence: Reflections on Father Daniel Berrigan
edited by Askold Melnyczuk

Ric's Progress by Donald Hall

Return To The Sea by Etnairis Rivera

The Kingdom of His Will by Catherine Parnell

Eight Notes from the Blue Angel by Marjana Savka

Fifty-Two by Melissa Green

Music In—And On—The Air by Lloyd Schwartz

Magpiety by Melissa Green

Reality Hunger by William Pierce

Soundings: On The Poetry of Melissa Green
edited by Sumita Chakraborty

The Corny Toys by Thomas Sayers Ellis

Black Ops by Martin Edmunds

Museum of Silence by Romeo Oriogun

City of Water by Mitch Manning

Passeggiate by Judith Baumel

Persephone Blues by Oksana Lutsyshyna

The Uncollected Delmore Schwartz
edited by Ben Mazer

The Light Outside by George Kovach

cont...

ARROWSMITH is named after the late William Arrowsmith, a renowned classics scholar, literary and film critic. General editor of thirty-three volumes of *The Greek Tragedy in New Translations*, he was also a brilliant translator of Eugenio Montale, Cesare Pavese, and others. Arrowsmith, who taught for years in Boston University's University Professors Program, championed not only the classics and the finest in contemporary literature, he was also passionate about the importance of recognizing the translator's role in bringing the original work to life in a new language.

Like the arrowsmith who turns his arrows straight and true,
a wise person makes his character straight and true.

— Buddha